The Great Scheme

David Bunn

The Great Scheme

Acknowledgements

'The Rockies' and 'Hallett's Peak' which appear within The Great Scheme poem sequence, were, in an earlier version, and as a single poem, shortlisted for the Blake Poetry Prize in 2012. That version is published by the NSW Writers Centre:
https://www.yumpu.com/en/document/read/52536421/once-upon-a-time-in-the-rockies.
Earlier versions of 'Erskine Falls' and the epigraph to The Great Scheme appeared during 2010 on a blog: 700verses.tumblr.com.
'Bad sky at night' was published in the *Australian Poetry Anthology* Vol. 8, 2020

In memory of Michele Turner and Susanne Whitlock

For my daughters Catherine, Jane and Anna

To Rosanne Cregan

The Great Scheme
ISBN 978 1 76109 198 8
Copyright © text David Bunn 2021
Cover image: Untitled, David Bunn 2019

First published 2021 by
GINNINDERRA PRESS
PO Box 3461 Port Adelaide 5015
www.ginninderrapress.com.au

Contents

Author's Note	7

The Great Scheme

1. God's waiting room	11
2. Among mountains	16
3. Over the lake	21
4. A case of gewürztraminer	28
5. Kooyong	32
6. In the stars	39
7. Mornington	45
8. Dark matter	49
9. Saint-Saturnin-lès-Apt	53
10. Sunshine Coast	58
11. Back Home	63
12. Great scheme	68
13. Mountain ash	73
14. Broken Head	77

Nothing but eternal peace

Bad sky at night	83
Who makes this stuff up?	84
Nothing but eternal peace	85
Pale cliffs	86
To RC framed in a prospect of vines	87
Limone	88
The trails above Castelletto	89
Mausoleum	90
Dante Square	91
In the springtime	92
Dream of defeat #23	93
A source	94

Faintest memory and lost causes	95
We owe him everything	96
Painting white	98
Ruination	99
We cannot say what it was	100
Flags	101
Meek man, no double	102
Religion and the second bass	103
Night, Córdoba	104
Il penseroso III	105
Bad night at Blois	106
Notes	108
About the Author	110

Author's Note

Recollection in tranquillity should be within my grasp. I have memories to burn: I have lived every year since the last world war. In my working life, I was fortunate enough to work for people and causes I believed in. I have tried to be of use.

The long sequence of poems, The Great Scheme, took shape in the years since 2016. The poems in the second part of the book, Nothing but eternal peace, span from 2013 to 2020.

With increasing dismay, I see chunks of my world slip below the horizon and out of the known universe. The facts will go on forever on huge databases, but not how these things were woven together as the fabric of our existence. That is where The Great Scheme started – trying to get that down.

Many thanks to these people who first read and responded to the poems in this book: Rosanne Cregan, Gabrielle Baldwin, Peter Fitzpatrick, Staś Hempel, John McLoughlin and Dugald Williamson.

The Great Scheme

When my endless talk of me is said and done,
when the flail has thrashed the ears to kingdom come,
when the final tempest bears off chaff and straw,
let's hope some grain gleams on the threshing floor.

1. God's waiting room

Holbrook

Bird-shit picnic tables, barbecue rotundas, is there
no better place to start than this highway stop in Holbrook?
Travelling children swarm about a scuppered sub
in the rolling inland, three hundred miles from sea.

A couple surface from their sardine-can sedan,
straighten their backs, get their legs used to land,
tartan thermos and Scotch fingers for their morning tea.

You made it! I greet them, gesturing with my wine sparkling.
You made it! Becoming a replica of my facetious dad –
not many believe that to reach Holbrook is to make it;
it's not like if you can make it here you can make it anywhere.

They drove from Canberra, you found out about their lives,
heading for Albury, not far in the great scheme of things,
and live in God's Waiting Room, a retirement home, they say.

*

God's Waiting Room they say, because it's a joke worth doing twice
and my reaction the first time was not adequately warm –
it's because they speak as though I'm knackered like themselves
and something flashed before my eyes from an unhappier time:

a happy hour and the pianist with dyed black hair and waxed
   eyebrows, playing
the hokey cokey and similar lewd songs like 'oh what a
   beauty!' and Sinatra songs,
and we have to stop whatever we're doing and say, 'what
   phrasing ol' blue eyes had!'
(like we never heard Jacques Brel or anyone who *cares* what
   they're singing)
and songs of longing like red sails in the sunset and harbour
   lights and the beguine.

Boiled cabbage and the clatter of prostheses are ineradicable
   on the air
and people, including my mother, sit waiting for their
   number to be called.

It's just an expression, I can hear you saying, and not to make
   too much of it,
but please, if I should ever mention that I'm waiting for a
   god, please
dispatch me in a cab to the Rationalistas to cop the contempt
   I deserve.

Red Sea

I went off subs one Sunday, sweating through a radio play
with dad, with a sub crew in the Red Sea, voices muffled,
with the sonar pinging around the echoing hull,
listening for a depth charge to tear the tin can apart
and the waters storming in to drown, like Pharaoh's army.

God's waiting room is that sub in the Barents Sea
settled on sea floor after an explosion, silent, without signal,
the survivors waiting in the last compartment for oxygen
to become exhausted and for the dark matter of death to
   crush in.

Runaway

An earth mover careered downhill like a runaway cable car
with people hanging off it, like an elephant rampage,
and trapped me under and crept, sensing my presence,
left me no way out, dodging the creaky moving parts.

I thought of nothing but to stay alive but still I was relieved –
this is what it's like, when the final moments come,
I do not suffocate from anguish, disintegrate; I will succumb
still absorbed by struggling to survive; terror regardless.

It's a dream, but in my sleep I spoke as if to waking me:
put aside your dread of the death, you will get through,
like you get through all else, and end;

and shakily my waking self replies, like
Camus' Meursault against the death sentence:

if it wasn't for the helplessness and

next breath not knowing if there is one

and on and on like that

Sault

This morning I dreamed you asked me to go down on you
(I can't find a way around this startling euphemism)
in an election tally room with counting soon to begin.
Already people with plastic names wandered through the room.

Outlandish, even in the dream I found it startling,
and definitely unsettling that you, a person of standing,
a woman of notable reserve and with gravitas to burn,
should ask this of me, a scruffy retiree, of no repute.

In your own dream you were feeling grateful that I'm good
at finding us some out-of-the-way spot in another country,
up early with the maps and tourist guides and phrase books,
plotting the route and how long it will take, while you dream.

I wanted to find out where in your dream I should take you.
It was important that you should say it was for pommes frites
on the summit of Mont Ventoux, with stalls of wooden crates
stacked high with brightly coloured confectionery and lozenges,

or the stop off in lovely Sault on the way back to Saint Saturnin,
where we persuaded a bar to give us baguettes and a beer
instead of closing for the day, which we ate outside a shop
with a sign for Huguenot funerals, wondering how they're different.

Coffin Villanelle

Do they address it like there's someone there inside,
beneath the closed lid, so they must raise their voice,
beneath the football scarf and the crumpled racing guide?

When it comes to this for me, my dearest bride,
if my residual pension covers a casket's price,
will you address it like there's someone there inside?

If you get a sense that I'm in there, open eyed
listening to you mourn, lying in solemn disguise,
beneath the football scarf and the crumpled racing guide,

taking a morbid pleasure and a kind of pride
in the fond words each survivor has devised
to address me like there's someone here inside

then take no chances, dear, let custom be defied,
open it and check if the life glints in my eyes
beneath the football scarf and the crumpled racing guide.

I may be screaming in the coffin there, beside
myself, wild to find I'll be one of those who dies
while folk address me like there's someone dead inside,
beneath the football scarf and the crumpled racing guide.

2. Among mountains

The Rockies

Denver may be outlaw as Kerouac suggests
but also blessed: over tattoo shops, light rail,
car parks, they beam dawn light through meagre air.

Children bicker in the back on who sits where,
when by some stage trick of perspective they're unveiled,
beyond the tawny foothills that we crawl through,
snow-capped rock, the crush of sky upon them.

My friend says Wordsworth's done it, and he has:
a dismal pinnacle rears as lustily he rows
an elfin pinnace down the midnight lake.

That does not blunt the shock of being
on the saddleback at fourteen thousand feet,
the light-filled air too fine for thought; being high
enough to face them face to blasted face;
being in their unmoved presence, in the bluster
and the blinding, in their encircling arc of might;
nor blunt the shock of this rough fact, raw stone.

They tell me that the natural won't suffice,
not even the natural sublime, and that
we live by meanings we have made, and yet
on those heights meaning's but a tattered coat
flapping sleeve-ends in the brutish gales.

Hallett's Peak

Below Hallett's Peak the pines surround Nymph Lake,
and in late afternoon they gather light
bright about its windswept bowl.
Lilies splotch the surface,
each pad's sallow windward flap
flips upright in the mountain gusts,
as though a fleet of slouch hats set sail,
or a flotilla of exotic yachts
tacked in thin sunlight for the prize;

or some deity devoted to this place
has lit her lamps and set them off to float,
each glowing like an elfin pinnace,
to grow in brightness as the dusk comes down,
and Hallett's Peak recedes to gloom.

Pretty Sally

As when a hiker who has pounded up a dragging slope,
intent on plodding, shrugging straps on aching shoulders,
breathing hard and staring hard at rough ground underfoot
so as not topple from a ledge or stumble on a stone,
and not to see the spirit-sapping distance still to climb,
scales the final rise and gasps, surprised to reach the end;

just as that walker attains the crest, without yet knowing it,
crosses the Great Divide and stares startled at the new terrain,
I looked up and found that folk had conquered overnight.
One moment it's Buddy Holly, Ricky Nelson, Marty Robbins,
each song brimful with teenage heartbreak, and the next
it's Odetta, Pete Seeger, Belafonte –

the names drag in a set from offstage and its lifelike props –
my parents' long-demolished living room, the radiogram,
guitars, harmonica and the wonky upright with its front off –
dad sings 'Frankie and Johnny' that he learnt before the war;
mum sings 'On the wings of a dove' she learned in church;
a wholesome time is had by all, including me, itching to rebel.

No white sports coat, no little wallflower on the shelf,
but jailbirds, drifters, maids and milk-white steeds;
Sir Patrick Spens and Pretty Boy Floyd; and the parting glass.
You're not who you thought, not a tag-along Top 40 kid,
but a boy with a guitar and a chord book and a hint
that your formless life is malleable to some purpose.

Mount Wellington

Trotsky lampoons the Tsar's diary, captured in the revolution:
'Walked long and killed two crows. Drank tea by daylight.'
'Got dressed and rode a bicycle to the bathing beach.'
Trotsky was astounded by his opponent's insouciance;
great and terrible events shake his Empire, while the Tsar
paddles his canoe; but for Nicholas this was life vibrant.

My mother climbed Mount Wellington to catch the dawn;
she needed us to see with her that first godly wash of rose,
faint on the far-flung Derwent and the eastern shore;
to see her world spread out before her at her wet-shod feet.
She needed us to know there was a world before us,
that there was a her; and I share her need to tell all I know:

How garbage men would run beside the slowly moving truck,
hoist cans on their shoulders and then upend them;
or how the iceman shouldered the glinting block of ice
and crashed it in the icebox and trimmed it with a pick
which is how Trotsky died in Mexico, or how in Carlton
I woke many a murky morning to the hooves of the milkman.

Gariwerd

There was a day I trudged the Grampians with my daughters
them ahead and going faster, gaining on me always,
uncertain in my footing, re-spending spent resources.

When we reached a summit with taller heights to either side,
a southern breeze breathed wide across the empty plains,
the land surveyed and pacified from range's foot to sea.

Since then I've read the map of massacres. I know that day
our conquering eyes traversed at least four killing sites,
and behind us in the valleys of the range were more.

Caught at each turn, I can't deny the tender awe
those cleared expanses, their dark windbreaks, inscribed
as signature upon the opened land, arouse in me, and yet

over there's the site with the poisoned flour, and there
by that far mount a raiding party sent to punish theft,
killed families and cleared them from their wooded lands.

My daughters, who brought me here, I bequeath you
this yearning to feel this outstretched land as ours
and the goading consequence of that cruel 'and yet'…

3. Over the lake

Whitehaven Beach

Last night she came to me – my dead wife appeared,
as she does from time to time, after twenty years of death.
I saw her doing yoga on a beach, straight backed,
her back turned to me, her face into brilliance.

Our daughter, still a child, plays about her in the sand
bathed by the radiance which flows around her mother,
or proceeds from her – air glows, she casts no shade.

She's like the young wife in *The Seventh Seal*
whose husband, the jongleur, watches from the trees
as she plays with their child in a sun-filled glade,
like an itinerant Madonna come to Sweden
with the plague.

This wife has the self-sufficient cool she always has in dreams,
and my daughter is engrossed in a wholehearted joy.
They don't know I exist.

                       I wake abashed before you,
my wife, for many reasons, including this grey-pink look
I have in the morning, as if someone coated me in cement
then thrashed me with a schnitzel;
but also because of my persistent dead.

*

The two dead women I wed before you stand behind you,
observing your baffled attempts to tend their children;
if you turn to them, they're not there, like a mirror
you pass in the dark and there's movement beside you,
but turn and there's shadow where there was flicker,
like bat wings in the vast figs on Rozelle Bay at midnight;
or in summer when the creek runs bright through scrub,
there's a shimmer above it, where mirage distorts the light,
causing the air to sway and blur, something on the edge
of perception, moving with the creek.

What you missed

You, the first, I see your look, the one in your portraits;
which shocks me when I pass you on our children's bookshelves;
your gaze confronting, sombre, but you also flinch from view;
I know my treachery before that photo, and what came after.

Those last years of the struggle in East Timor – at the end
the pro-Indo militias off the leash, in a brutal hounding
assault to punish the people for voting independence,
and to leave it gashed and bleeding when they left –

You missed those years and those last insupportable months;
how could you have survived that lacerating helplessness?
You had no way to shut the terror out that others suffered,
it came screaming into you and you screamed.

*

It's different now. We turn back refugees at sea or maroon
the ones who reach us on distant tropical islands,
and the children too, left without a possible hope.
You have missed this; you are not implicated in this.

You would be driven to another desperate misery,
you would search for an act of outrageous extremity,
to convince us this could not be supported;
as though we did not know, and you had to jolt us;

because we alternate between an anaesthetic blankness,
and a state of despairing futility, between getting on with life
and guilt for our crimes of omission and complicity,
between our grandchild to come and the despair in the camps.

You would not alternate, everything would clash together;
you would not be good at getting to sleep at night
while others are frightened or starving, running or weeping,
but this is a skill we need in our country at night,

            to get to sleep.

You should have been here

Xanana brought you a medal to Melbourne
and your daughters received the award on your behalf.
He is a very inspiring man, as you would have expected;
you could tell from the way he was with our daughters,
the respect, the regard, the acknowledgement of their loss –
I never saw anyone with his astounding depth of being.
But what point describing him? You should have been here.

You should have been here to see your daughters,
who were entirely his equals, upright and excellent,
none finer, none straighter, none more graciously solemn;
steadfastly loyal, with you and without you.

*

You snuck in and stood behind my shoulder
as I watched our flautist daughter play a concert,
and I had to mutter to you as we watched her

– You see that intensity she got from you?
How she takes on Messiaen, flat out, front on,
with my borrowed chopsticks knotted in her hair?

Now that her solo's been practiced for weeks,
that blackbird infesting my narrow sounding house,
you reckon you can sidle in to see her perform,

where on earth do you think you have been? –
I turned to face you and you turned away
with a hint of a smile in the gloom of the hall.

You who had been fearless, would stop at nothing,
leapt tiny on a stage to harangue Gough Whitlam,
and the High Court judge with him, would not answer.

*

You will become a grandmother. Our daughter,
staunch and pragmatic, cannot sort the emotions
that are bound up in this, that you will miss her child
and her child miss you and there is no sorting of it.
You should have been here.
                                  As much as we tell ourselves
that you did not choose to leave, that you had no choice,
as much as we tell ourselves that, again and again,
I will think it persistent – you should have been here.

Night after night

And you, the second, in that powder blue windcheater,
or green Fair Isle jumper or blue T-shirt shimmering on mauve
with your hair cut short, or head shaved during chemo,
or the tight curls that grew back after chemo wore off,
we know about getting to sleep at night while death knocks
on the bedroom door.
                          How could I live without you?
I muttered late one night seized by the darkest goading,
and you, silently lying awake in ambush, murmured
that's your problem, buster, your voice low and slurred
and I lay there a long time trying to unsay our words.

Night after night I slept beside you, struggling
to forget what must happen.
                        Two years and more,
the tumours advancing and receding, never out of the woods,
from city to city, from one house to another, in flight.
A few years we were raised up and then brought low.

If you arrived

If you allowed yourself to come on this soft air,
moving as it gently wills, drifting without volition
from your cool world to this humid press of night;
and if with me you gazed into my long house,
into that room with our books mixed on the shelves
with hers who rests on the couch her sleeping head,
distant in the lamp glow as in a Dutch interior,
my wife, who by ill chance you cannot meet
although she's raised your girl these many years,
though you could not find a friend more loyal,
if you arrived with this sweet cool breath of air.

She moved through the fair

Back in the folk days, when I was a hopeful boy,
on a library shelf of songs, I found a song whose worth
I would not attempt to weigh for forty years, although
I knew it was beyond my weighing from the start:

> She turned away from me and she moved through the fair
> and fondly I watched her move here and move there,
> and she started homeward with one star awake,
> as the swan in the evening moves over the lake.

A doctor friend told me about pneumonia and similar conclusions –
the frontal lobe shuts down, it's starved of oxygen, he said.
It is a comfort. The patient not fully conscious, does not know
that her end is approaching.

It was relevant, you had spent your last night without me.
I went home to feed the children and didn't come back
until morning. Something happened to my frontal lobe,
and I didn't come back until morning.

4. A case of gewürztraminer

Old Arts

Fifty years ago, as so much is, a grey afternoon,
aloft with the Moreton Bay fig luxuriant outside
the window of your office in Old Arts, which is now
a magnolia or camellia; but you're not there to ask;

your Senior Service smouldering in your hand, the flesh
a little puffy at your wrist, swollen, as if by illness,
like it would be tender to the touch, you lean back and turn
a disenchanted gaze towards the fading light and say
that at your age when you question someone's motives
you are bound to arrive at a cynical answer.
                                              You were 43,
I figure from your birthdate in your *Collected Poems*,
and I was 21; mixed teenage cynicism with my gloom.

Of all I know you said, and wrote, that sentence was mine,
said to me alone, which I've quoted these last fifty years.
I had a teacher once, I say to some stuck person, and he said –
question someone's motives you're sure to come up cynical…

to get them to move on, to leave tangled rumination
like a twisted ball of twine, to do whatever must be done.

Each time I say it I think – you were urging me to move on,
but from what I should move on, I cannot reconstruct.

'We need people like you here' you said, and ever since
I've wondered what sort of people you thought I am like.

I heard you once describe yourself as syndicalist,
in a sprawling conversation around a cafeteria table,
about the need not to be corralled with the Right,
condemned to be capitalist because we were anti-Soviet.
I went off to search out what 'syndicalist' meant and found
Lenin condemning labourism, and Orwell saw it working
in Catalonia, and I ended up working forty years in Unions.
With no prior warning that I was a person like that.

Catalonia

When Orwell went to Barcelona to write about the Spanish war
the waiters refused tips; the cafés were under workers' control
and the tramways. It was a strange state of affairs and disconcerting
but one that was evidently worth defending, so he joined a militia.

I have told his story many times as if it was my moment of courage,
his decision to enter the fray, not to stand on the sidelines,
and I've halted the telling to hide my sob at what a decent
   bloke he was,
and what a decent bloke I must be, to remember and tell his story.

*

That lad we met in France who'd hiked from Munich on his own,
who said he was less lonely on the trails than he'd been at home,
was moving fast. By now he will have crossed the breadth of Spain
where pilgrims can choose their way, but not the Catalans.

Bochara

Geoff, jocose at cellar door, showed off his wines and then
his model railway – a bamboozling replica of Somerset;
goods and mainline and local trains at the flick of a switch.

The nearest I'd ever seen was the control room for the railways
where technicians worked a console, which showed the network
as grand scheme, with individual trains displayed as moving lights.

I stood there in easy reach of the dials and buttons
with the driverless lights careering and dodging near-misses
at junctions; and it was like looking down on creation.

His wife grew up in Somerset whilst he grew among the sheep
of New Zealand; and I don't know where their lights converged,
but he's ended with a good train set and a share of a vineyard.

At 70 you seize what you have to hand – tracks and rolling stock,
a case of gewürztraminer. You say, Look what I have wrought.

Fontvieille

Beneath the tumbled aqueduct French insects whirr.

Carpenters and masons, labourers and water boys
would wake to building arches and they'd gauge
the leagues from here to distant Arles and mutter:
   Two thousand of these bastards left to build.
   I know that I am still of use.

I'm turning into *Three Sisters* or is it *The Cherry Orchard?* –
in a billabong becalmed by pointlessness, although
I've tried to be of use, as useful as you can
when you're neither nurse nor vigneron.

If this were chess, then I am in time trouble.
I am running out of it while black fate stares me
out across the board. I can't see a step ahead,
while she calmly deploys a hundred hinted threats.

5. Kooyong

Polling booth

A bitter curse upon winter elections
and any warm-wrapped silvertail who calls them, in the dark
overcoats that make our betters look like stockbrokers;
and curse outdoor trade union rallies, with Trotskyists queuing
for the frozen mike so it takes all afternoon to get to the pub;
and all-night picket lines in the rain and briquette smoke.

Outside the polling booth we do four hours freezing for the cause,
where conservatives have gathered in well-spoken hordes,
with their accents you must admire, for which their parents paid
and paid, which would be their own affair if only they didn't claim
a plug of my tax to help their offspring get ahead of mine
in the queue for degrees and wealth and well-being,
and then insist that people in the camps must wait their turn.

It's a mystery to us opponents why they bother at this place.
Tectonic plates will crack and suck Kooyong to perdition
before the ruling class will lose this seat.

                                            I guess they huddle
around an assured victory as though around a fire, to feel like winners,
like those shallow boys who choose which football team to follow
from among the most successful teams as they grow up
and figure they'll always be assured of coming out on top.

*

The young woman here for the Greens will not stop talking
with the Tory gaggle. I've been doing this too long, I know
that even when they are personally pleasant and even good,
and follow forlornly the same abject football team you do,
the blue bloods are still full of the servant problem and strikes
and unions, penalty rates and overtime and how a century ago
there might have been exploitation but now they're pampered –
those uncouth toilers who make their coffee and clean their sewers,
and in defiance of Newton the pendulum has swung too far.

She teeters on the edge of arguing for a test of mental competence
to get the vote, because if you can't put four numbers in order
with a pencil on a piece of paper then surely you don't deserve
anyone's sympathy and you may not deserve the right to vote.
Which sets the superior Liberal into a rant on voluntary voting –
if you're too stupid to want to vote then no one should make you.
I think of a worker I know, with an intellectual impairment,
who would as likely cast a wise vote as these literate fools.

The two of them are too young to think back seventeen years,
(when did everything get to be so long ago?) they don't remember
East Timor, when voters who didn't know if militia would attack,
and may not have been able to read or write to save themselves,
stood in lines for many hours to vote for independence.

Red

Once I used to care about the lovely earth –
stood four-square with the Club of Rome,
and with Robert Lowell I pitied the planet,
'all joy gone from this sweet volcanic cone'.

Clear-felling
dismayed me in the Otways, where I drove a million years ago
in an Austin 30, with a wonky link from throttle
to carburettor, which I fixed with chewing gum one hot day,
before global warming; and I still believe in dystopia to come
when we are forced to eat a loathsome plankton-swill, concoct
in huge vats, like at the school-lunch factory I saw in Japan;
and we hide in stacked ant colonies terrified of air outdoors,
and the best and bravest of us refuse the order to procreate
on pain of death, because our children would never see the sky,
and to put an end to this Ponzi scheme called growth;
but nowadays I note how every good environmental deed
costs some poor sucker I don't know their job – far off
from our barista-crowded suburbs stuffed with the high-minded,
who won't suffer if the mines should close or logging stop,
who can move their money on when steel towns rust.

I don't flirt with Green; I keep faith
with my cranky version of the Red.

Pillar of smoke

It was a plan of grinding simplicity – follow the pillar of
 smoke by day
for forty years, wherever it led, no matter how dry the gulches,
with the rulers hostile when they condescended to notice,
and the locals, cowed and tormented, suspicious.
Wherever you went it was always ahead of you.

At night, as a pillar of fire, it stood outside camp, glowering,
silent, not like those beacon fires some of our ancestors built
to bring news roaring at night of the coming of Spain or Napoleon,
not the glare of disaster on the belly of clouds in our fire season;
this stood still in the wildest weather, and had only one meaning –
tomorrow the whole solemnly prolonged thing was there to
 be done again.

There may be no why to it, it is notoriously difficult to work
 out motives,
especially one's own – it's hard to remember or admit the
 tangled confusion
which made it impossible to decide on a course, and then in
 frustration
there comes the moment when you say fuck it and start off,
 come what may.
There's always post facto fudging to pretty things up, to draw lines
between dots as if that was where you always were heading, and that
was where you were coming from and the whole shambling
 thing made sense,
was always the noblest of callings despite the slipshod look,
and the dubious outcomes.

Each morning there was the pillar of smoke.

If only it was clear at the start that it was to be forty years of wandering,
and that the end would be a state of affairs no better
than how things were at the start, or worse; and if we'd been warned
that we'd cover the same ground often, the same trip over and over,
each time certain we would get it right this time; and if we knew
our attempts to organise ourselves for the trek and choose our leaders
would be unpicked and resewn in rancour, as if each previous version
was the work of fools and had always been bound to fail, although
we were those fools redoing what we had done as best we could;
if only we foresaw that our disputes about principles and ends,
about matching our methods of work to our goals and vice versa,
would be repeated for forty years with growing weariness,
with the factions swapping positions but maintaining enmity,
with each victory exposing another weakness on a forgotten flank,
and what we built and accomplished beginning to crumble
before we drank the dedicatory toasts and read our speeches,
we might have struck out, tried our luck without the pillar,
straightforwardly doing the same worthwhile thing, year after year,
but without our delusion that each act was the start of something better.

Orwell still

One of my girls is travelling, maybe in Spain, maybe north of Nice;
she's a long way off this election day, and I think of her,
her bleak answer before she left, when I quoted Orwell:[1]

> I don't know that Orwell imagined just how bad it would get.
> I think it goes well beyond jobs and a roof that doesn't leak.
> My children will face an almost uninhabitable world.
> We're not going to have enough clean oxygen or space or water.
> I don't know if we can imagine just how bad it will get.

In my antiquated way I would like to see her in a steady job,
not this casual, half-arsed, freelance stuff they sell the young
as freedom, which barely keeps the wolf from their doors.
And right now, she has a roof that doesn't leak, for which
I am glad, and she's perhaps not adequately grateful,
and we can't imagine how bad things were when Orwell wrote;
but I agree with her, and it's not only a matter of how bad
it will get, but also what sort of bad, that we can't imagine.

My country

The missionary youth tend their sausage barbecue,
bunting flutters, wind rattles the last plane-tree leaves,
a distant train departs, rumbling from the nearest station.
From long ago some words of Randy Newman's rise:
*This is my country, these are my people, and I know them
like the back of my own hand.* On and on in my head,
a satire that sounds genuine and sad the more you sing it.
My country, my people?
                      Insensible, self-deceived,
consumed with contention while the earth cracks beneath
   our feet?
Country which is ours through two centuries of grasping?

It's cold, it rains; it's mid-afternoon and the unwilling drizzle
of voters stops. The traffic stops, the Green stops provoking
the conservatives who stop, for a moment, talking about their
   dogs.
You are at the other gate, conversing with some stranger there.
A bird moves cautious in the leaves, and silence falls.

6. In the stars

Astor Bar

Have you heard it's in the stars? Next July we collide with
 Mars.
Cole Porter got it. We die, swell, there's a celestial plan.
But who can believe it, their cocktail in their hand?
Well did you evah! they say. What a swell party this is!

That song is this side of an event horizon, before it there's a
 black hole
sucking my life backwards to it: a yellow tip-truck, a sandpit,
a Christmas tree, a burglary, the cockatoo in the shop next door,
an ice cream factory with padded men, like spacemen, in the cold.

Atomic Bunn my parents called me – an afterglow from
 events before me.
I was active and destructive and born in '46 and fondly
they nicknamed me after Hiroshima and Nagasaki;
unfeeling it seems now, with tens of thousands killed;

but that was the plan, that was in my stars, to press on lamenting
my yellow truck, despite the misfortunes of millionss.

Cairo

Mimsie Starr got mysteriously pinched in the Astor Bar
which must be like the casbah where your father went in Cairo,
when he fought the Germans and got sick mending planes,
and came home with a brass gong for his mother.

Hard to imagine your father bargaining in the bazaar,
clean cut and far from home, with stubbled native craftsmen
squatting at a work bench, in some strange broken language,
gouging brass with a mallet and graver for tourist-soldiers.

It was strange the way your father said casbah or baksheesh –
as if he held them between thumb and a finger at arm's length,
because they were the unpleasant words of the Egyptian fellahin,
who were themselves disturbing and like their tongue distasteful.

You weren't there, his tone stressed that, you were missing,
you would never be that young man far from home,
among strangers who he knew meant him no good.
That tone was as close as he got to telling me he was scared.

Then he got his ulcer which we know now is *helicobacter pylori,*
but it could have been rotten water or food, or the deaths of
   his pilots,
or the fear of being buried alive in a slit trench under bombing,
or the effort of staying upright in a hostile land, to get through.

Bealiba Times

My visiting grandfather declared he heard me shout,
as I raised rebellion under the willow in the front yard,
Viva Khrushchev! not long after he denounced Stalin.

My dad denounced his father for perverse stupidity.
No child of his was a friend of Khrushchev. But I've thought since
Grandad heard me shouting what he wanted me to shout.

He sounds like he was a great socialist – a utopian Fabian
from the nineteenth century like George Bernard Shaw,
dedicated to Darwin and to world peace through Esperanto,

but fifty years before Khrushchev the *Bealiba Times*
records his speech in the Great War, at a public meeting,
for conscription in the referendum, because he says

all his kin of military age are in the trenches and, too old to go
himself, he must do whatever he could to support them
(by sending others' sons – his own being happily too young).

Maybe the Great War was just, and conscription not wrong –
but Grandad turns out to be a disappointing radical, like me –
jostled by time and circumstance from high-flown beginnings.

Per Ardua

Per ardua ad astra. By struggle to the stars.
Per ardua ad astra – each human step was proof –
to launch weather balloons swelling to the stratosphere,
and bounce short waves back from the ionosphere,
and hear Test cricket whooshing in and out of phase
from England; to hear a jet break the barrier of sound
and then Roger Bannister breaks the four-minute mile;
and to stand on the dark front lawn with your children
and watch sputnik feebly streak across the skies;
to survive till space boots kick up moon glow;
to catch the fleeting streak of particles in cloud chambers –
each stoked Dad's certainty that everything gets better,
that progress is unquenchable as gravity, that it draws us
upwards to unconquered summits which, once conquered,
must be surpassed and he'd shake his head and say,
in a kind of doting amazement, where will it ever end?

TPI Sestina

I lost the lottery this fellow won,
I see he's got a TPI badge on his jacket –
Totally and Permanently Incapacitated.
They pulled his birthday marble from a barrel
and all his Christmases had come at once:
conscription to Vietnam was the prize.

I was in that sweepstake but didn't gain a prize;
my number wasn't drawn so what I won
was a lucky life, a healthy one; not once
forced into armour instead of duffel jacket,
never ordered to stare down a gun barrel
not Temporarily or Partly Incapacitated.

The once I could have been incapacitated
I was knocked off a Vespa, out cold like a prize
fighter, arse over tit, lock stock and barrel.
The old bloke in the slowly moving car who won
that unequal bout, leaving on his jacket,
not even raising a sweat, was maybe young once.

No thanks to him I too survived to be young once,
they scraped me off the road, incapacitated
but only for five minutes, my body with its jacket
of tar, my Vespa fit to enter in a sculpture prize
for misshapen objects, which it would have won,
like a Spitfire which fails to complete a barrel

roll and ends up a heap of rubble and a barrel
of unidentified metal oddments which had once
been a lad in a very fast plane who could have won
a battle in his glory days, incapacitated
with no hope of gaining the mark or winning the prize;
clad in earth instead of his pilot's leather jacket.

My dad wore no TPI badge on his jacket
to signify that his life had not been a barrel
of laughs; he didn't join groups, did not prize
the company of those he'd fought with once,
did not seek out his fellow incapacitated;
he sat tight in the house that his War Service won.

Unlike this bloke he tried to shed his war like a jacket once
his ulcer got him over a barrel, got him incapacitated
out, took his spleen as initial prize, and finally won.

7. Mornington

Ringer

My border collie with the white band circling your black
right wrist, you would trot, head high, up the sandy track
to survey your extensive domain and then set to work,
as if that were your job, herding sheep in the paddock.

Next there's a farmer threatening to shoot the bloody dog
the next time. I see him wave his rifle at our door,
but that can't be right, that cannot possibly be right
this was our sleepy seaside village, not Fitzroy;
it's one of those moments more garish than the truth –
like when I saw the Beagle Boys, in their jailbird pyjamas,
running from my parents' shop after a smash and grab,
or when I saw the body of a man run over in Punt Road,
purple in the mercury vapour streetlights,
as the ambulance crew rolled him in a blanket.
Both times my parents told me that could not be right;
but although I was supposed to, I could not forget.

*

One day that dog barks damned near all night, and next day
he drags me along a fox's trail, the paw prints running
for a mile along the flat topped raised-earth rampart
where the sewer was laid, and then the clay backfilled.
It was one of those rare moments where you both want
exactly the same thing – to catch the fox, which had priors,
having taken the heads off our hens on another raid.
But we'd never catch him before I went to school.

Salt wind

Up the hill a pair of spindly she-oaks inclined mournful at a dam,
filled in when the high school was built, only to be pulled down,
where I suffered weekly humiliation on the sporting fields,
the dismissive disregard of the cool girls (who'll look as old
as me now, if they're lucky) magpies swooping in nesting season,
foxtrot lessons in the woodwork room before school dances.
Nothing lasted longer, it turns out, than the lonesome moan
of wind among the dusty needles of the she-oaks
on a gasping hot day, sounding like a blizzard in the Yukon,
like the storm that swept away everything before us.

*

Beneath the settlers' orchards and their staggering shacks;
under the paddocks and then the housing estate;
along the melaleuca verges of the tidal creeks
or on the distance-hazy slopes of hills called mounts,
another world lay, ransacked.

                      At school we learned
there were Aboriginal people at Sorrento and Geelong
who Buckley lived among, a tall white commanding respect
among the tribes, but for me that was school stuff,
like they were not people, as boring as kings and queens,
picturesque subjects crouching in pitiable gunyahs.

Walk the clifftop paths and your sandshoes scuffled
the edges of a midden, the shell fragments scattered bright,
like mother of pearl inlay in the pale sandy earth,
but I didn't know that yet, looked to my feet for snakes.
We were rootless people, nostalgic about half a century –
antique bottles clinked as we dug our veggie patches,
provoking a thrill of imagination, who had preceded us? –
But the people who worked and named the land for millennia
did not exist for us when we asked that question,
were no more our predecessors than the creatures they hunted.

That gale that scoured our memory, like salt wind crumbling
the timber of a boat house by the sea, whirled off those prior
so that our mild peninsula, its slopes greening with vines,
its waters relentlessly ploughed by the wake of pleasure craft,
its roads and bistros full of us, the wilfully forgetful,
is not disturbed by the facts of encroachment, dispossession.

Saturdays

Juniors played for free on Saturdays on the golf course
and my mate and I played with his mother's clubs,
growing hungry as we went, him compact and able,
and me from rough to rough, all over the place.
We drove towards the sea and the fairway on the sixth
ran along the cliffs, where the salt wind whipped us,
like we stood somewhere forlorn in the Outer Hebrides.

That country, with the rich houses below the brow of the hill
and up here the sea striking bright and hard into your eyes,
made you feel lonely in the sunshine, with your best mate there,
on the great windswept slope, under a wide indifferent sky.
We were small creatures moving slowly across a vast space,
into a blessed hollow out of the wind, or up the blustery slope
of a gully, and we went without trace, like floating in nothing.

The midden builders could recall in their legends
when the Yarra ran through its broad valley to the Heads.
The people stood on those cliffs and the bush around them
cascaded with sounds they had heard for thousands of years;
the gullies had names, the hilltops had names, and they watched
the waters rising after the Ice Age to fill the valleys they'd tended.

What the lightning said

Ringer trotted off to a Gippsland farm and was killed
by lightning as he ran beside the farmer's tractor,
I was told, but marvelled that the farmer was not struck.
Then I convinced myself the big tyres saved him.
But now I think that the lightning is a euphemism
for putting my dog down – another euphemism in itself.
I suspect a kind mendacity in my mother – and now
I will have to rethink those dashing Beagle Boys
and the man run over in Punt Road near Commercial,
opposite the hospital where my daughter works,
who I confidently expect will be a kindly lying mother.

8. Dark matter

Cannaregio

We came from Murano on the wrong *vaporetto*
and trod fuzzily home to Ghetto Nuovo in the still,
with each border sharply marked – our side of the canal
in light and the opposite in shadow, and each ledge,
capstone and cobble edged by a shade precisely drawn.

I began the walk disgruntled because of the wrong ferry,
and because I found Murano in autumn oppressive,
with no buyers of the glass and many gloomy sellers,
and the canal down the middle as empty and forbidding
as a Bertolucci set where some evil must befall.

Then I looked from our sunlight along a gloomy lane,
and in the sunlight at the other end, along a parallel canal,
a boatman standing at the tiller of his barge processed
through the frame in silence, his gaze cast forward on the water,
distant as a doge's portrait glimpsed through an arch.

Creswick

Today at Creswick woollen mill they talk to me as if I'm human,
not the dopey aged specimen they see in me in town;
straightforward country girls tempt me to spend a fortune
and then they study Derrida and marketing on weekdays.

Then to the museum where history begins with the gold rush
and 50,000 years of past has disappeared without a mention;
it's gripped by bark huts, mullock heaps, shafts and a tragic flood,
which leaves no room for conquest and dispossession.

Then off to a winery which the French built on conquered land
provoking the locals who think we should drink native;
but if the French are prepared to serve us cheese and wine
on our weekend away, we respond with jail-break elation.

Drive back through wide-open country under gathering dusk –
I photograph a ruined hut behind a pair of crude-hacked pines.
There's an old flatbed wagon upslope in a stand of tangled trees,
and I feel kinship with these ugly weather-bashed survivors.

The whole day the clouds have barely changed – high above
   cold country,
with bright captivating wisps in front of dull and darker backdrops.
It's like watching a slow earthquake from a soundproof booth;
oblivious as dark matter, they sail remote as Venetian barges.

Dark matter

On the other side, in the dark matter universe, have they
figured out that a working universe requires more
than all the dark matter put together can amount to,
and do they have the same problem detecting us as we do them?

Their dark universe must be drenched with an astonishing
effulgence for which they can find no source, nor cause:
an all-pervading light which blasts the possibility of shade,
it beams into them from our unimaginable dimension.

A dark matter woman, with her dark power, must willy-nilly
use her powers for darkness, as best as she can, although
she be a woman without shadow, while in our opposite world
I am stuck with light, for good or ill, in dapple and in dark.

Like bishops of opposite colours in the hands of opponents
we can stand side by side and have no effect on the other,
our fields of force go forth without alteration or mingling,
I cannot take her, nor she take me, nor can we ever touch.

In bundling, that enlightened backwoods courtship practice,
the couple, with no contract signed nor troth plighted,
is put to bed with a sheet between them, not to be dislodged,
and pass the night exploring surfaces of each other,

which is what Henry VIII should have done instead
of sending Holbein to gauge the comeliness of Anne of Cleves.
But even separated by that sheet a couple would be closer
than we are to our magic doubles in the darkling universe.

Eurydice

Things were unwell between us, I kept on shouting
that you hated my company. You didn't say so,
but I knew that I was lost if I kept up shouting.
I went out on foot, with a notion you might follow,
up the hill in the gloomy light shed by a tall forest
which let nothing grow beneath it and with the walk
my mood expanded; I reached a crest with a better nature.

You must have gone downhill instead of climbing with me,
and I gazed down the aisles of trees and dun earth expanses
into gloomy valleys, but I could not see you there below.
You answered your phone before I rang. You were lost.
I heard somebody with you ask if you knew where to go,
and you said you came from up the hill, from Lorna Doom,
which alarmed me – that's not a town but a history novel.

Something woke me before I could find you and I must search –
the woods outside Bonn, the coastal redwoods in Marin County,
the Edenic plantations we rode through on the Loire,
the untouched stands of mountain ash towards the Otways,
the dry ironbark tracks at the back of Airey's Inlet,
and nothing I could think of was like the forest in my dream.
It may not be real that forest and I might never find you.

I'm doing the dishes when I recall where I've seen that forest –
It's those hillsides where lyrebirds rake the soil to feed –
and whole slopes can look like they're weeded and mulched.
You, my Eurydice, you are only a Sunday drive away,
close by Belgrave Station, but lost in hilly folded landscape –
and I am that many-voiced Orpheus who lost you,
looking foolishly backwards and downwards into dimness.

9. Saint-Saturnin-lès-Apt

Vaucluse

Remember looking from the escarpment towards Nowra,
the Pacific a glinting ribbon on the fading high horizon,
the way the underpinning curving of the land is jammed
into the unbending coercions of colonial surveyors?

No surveyor conceived this valley with its agricultural lots,
its horticultural parcels – vines and olive groves and orchards
bounded by windbreaks, and the routes marked by spires
of blue-dark pines. I see why Cézanne said he saw in patches.

The road with our stone cabin in it climbs towards the church
whose steeple is level with us here, where we stand by ruins.
We are taken up unto a high place and have the goodly world
spread out before us – the fair folded fields of Provence.

Memorial

It's market day: canvas parasols, refrigerated vans,
olives, cheeses, sausage, money changing hands,
the trickle of the fountain muffles voices at the stalls.
You shop and I wait in the plane-tree shaded square
of our village-for-a-week; I slump and read the wall –
memorial to fourteen dead in occupied Vaucluse.

Fourteen marble blocks pattern paler local stone;
on each block there's a name (where the name is known).
Most of them came from elsewhere in Provence
but some of the dead came far to die that day –
Robert the Belgian (who has no family name),
one from Montparnasse, one from the Forbidden Zone.

Blanche Gaillard was local; she died on her farm at Berre,
a few kilometres away, but she was buried here
in town – an uplands farmer with her photo on her grave,
with her husband who'd been dead about five years,
and one of their sons is with them, who also *Died for France,*
six years after she died, in a colonial war, I guess.

Four of the fourteen were shot against this wall
executed in the early afternoon, beneath this tall,
impervious sky, at the hushed centre of the hillside town.
The plane trees and fountain rustled here the day they died
but not the market, not the vendors, not the hum of daily life –
not the lightness of buying, of drinking, of waking the next day.

Berre

Blanche *Died for France*, her gravestone says, and where she died,
but her place at Berre is hard to find; it is a speck
on a large-scale map and we're nearly skittled by a mower
on the way, hacking back the hedges on the narrow lanes.

Blanche sheltered young men on her farm, including a son,
resisters and fugitives from compulsory labour in the Reich.
On moonlit nights they gathered and hid about the farm
war supplies dropped by bombers flying from Tangiers.

When we get there, the way is barred with a high fence,
and a sign that looks like it means business warns
of savage dogs; but the Germans found their way,
directed by an informer who had earlier passed by.

At dawn a German column attacked a camp of fugitives nearby
then sent a squad up the rough track to the farm at Berre;
with two of her children by her they shoot Blanche at her door,
while her oldest son with his comrades watched from the scrub.

The résistant poet René Char describes an abysmal day
with the young men at his side pleading that he must launch
an attack, while the safety of their village required
they stay still, hold fire, and watch a comrade die:

> He fell as though he did not notice his executioners,
> and so lightly that it seemed to me that the slightest
> breath of wind must lift him from the ground.
> I did not give the signal because the village must be spared
> at any cost. What is it but a village, like all the rest?[2]

Morts et mortes pour la France

Or was it for Vaucluse they died? That land,
whether they fled here or were bred here,
took them to itself, encompassed them.

It never asked them if they belonged,
never promised them an even break,
but claimed them, took them as its own.

We climbed past the ruined fort and on,
the valley and blue folded ranges at our back,
to the memorial on the cliff at Romanet.

Remember us, it says, the five who died
in summer darkness here, the two unknown,
and Isaac Malho, Albert Rouzeau, Maurice Barthou

who whether they knew it or not
died for this country, these rock uplands
entangled in the tang of wild thyme.[3]

Promenade des Anglais, Nice

Here it is – a blurry photo taken on a day the US brass
decorated résistants with a Medal of Freedom,
for services rendered to downed Allied airmen,
on the seafront at Nice, arrayed in wavering lines.

Two brothers whose mother Blanche was shot at her farm,
up towards Ventoux, while one watched from the scrub;
and Juno, motor mechanic and *maire* standing near
who led the teams to gather parachuted supplies and arms;

and Archiduc who directed them in that task,
who was, he told René Char, a banterer, suspicious,
poisoned by insincerity, until he joined the résistance –
but was now direct, engaged, an alchemist, said Char.

Terrorists the Germans called them, terrorists said
the collaborators and the people looking for a quiet life;
and a cause is not proven just because it enlivens,
gives direction and purpose, the worst cause can do that.

The line of people staggers towards the sea, becomes blurrier;
there are women in the formation towards the other end,
but not staunch Blanche Gaillard killed at her remote farm,
and then American troops in a kind of honour guard.

Amongst the résistance crimes I've seen recorded –
the destruction of aluminium smelters outside Avignon
informers assassinated, trains sabotaged, abductions –
there was no plot to drive a truck into a crowd.

   16 March 1947–Bastille Day 2016

10. Sunshine Coast

Above Toulouse

On the upper of Elantxobe's two main streets
we cross paths with a local and I nod *¡Hola!*
He lumps us with the conquering Spaniards.
We get nothing save a blank Basque glare.

But in France I walk the trails with easy mind,
no dispossessed claimant to cause unease,
the only trace of first peoples is in the caves,
or in our genes as undeciphered legacy.

One time, at least, the English took our town,
or mercenaries set loose by a bankrupt prince,
and then in the square where we drank white wine
the Huguenots brought in and murdered 90 priests.

But no claim upon me, no shadow at my back,
whatever fell out here can't be pinned on me.
It all went down without me, a long time ago –
the tides of ice advanced and then withdrew.

Mount Ngungun

We are climbing Mount Ngungun which is sacred, perhaps
a divinity, like all mountains I suppose, though I know little
of mountains. We are asked not to climb to the summit,
not to place ourselves above other beings, mortal or immortal.

Mount Ngungun is the mild attendant of the Glasshouse
    Mountains,
the great ones, a humble witness to their might, and we scale
its lesser heights to stare upon them in their grave assembly,
and how the patterned farmlands draw back at their skirts.

Up the breakneck steeps is tough, tumbled rocks for path;
below, a bone-crushing fall into the bouldered crevasse.
When we stop to grasp for breath, we also catch the view –
blue veiled they maintain momentous impassivity.

Each stands in its own field of force, each an ageless power:
the hunched beast that bars the way southward; the crooked
pinnacle to the west, bare rock thrust beyond green shoulders,
bright until it drowns in shadow from its great mother
    further west.

Climbers press past us, shouting. As if this land is theirs,
laid on for their conquest; they race to the peak and triumph
taunting heaven, as though they had never heard of respect,
as though we were not born to fear and awe and silence.

The tick of the human

A scrawny preacher takes as his text a quote
he claims is from my former tutor – 'Only
the human tick can register the tick of the human' –
which to a Sunday painter makes a sort of sense.

It's many years since this tutor taught me
and I don't know that she ever spoke that phrase;
it looks awkward, like something you invent
in a dream, but she could have meant it.

I remember her upturned hand swung in an arc
closed, then open, then closed again, like small
explosions or like water lilies spreading wide,
registering something Gerard Manley Hopkins did.

She taught me literature, may have taught me
that use of 'register' – that act of openness
as an artist performs their art, almost instinct,
the way the world presses upon the wrists,

how dusk chills a gallery where women come and go,
and the gleam of a silk dress slithers in pearl light;
the wondering regard of a watcher from a parapet
as autumn overwhelms a valley with a swirl of mist.

Currumundi

It's like awakening in a distant land, except
you recognise the language and the brands
on shelves, but the townships are all beautiful –
Pacific Haven, Pelican Waters, Little Cove –
as if a speculator's publicist had written them.

On the beach the generations come and go,
cluttering the brochures' unspoiled sands,
from the ramp at the bottom of our street
to the tidal inlet that the locals call the lake;
figures become smudges in the ocean haze.

They are rugged against what they think is winter,
following their jolly dogs, whirling plastic slings
and balls to fetch, but sometimes there's a tern
or a shag, and today an osprey perched nearby
called a warning to her children sporting in a creek.

Half a million dead in Syria, they said last night,
but how do they count? It's hard to find someone
who's not to blame; dead parents and their children,
an infant generation who barely stood before they died,
who got no chance to fight in their own civil war;

they are pierced by poison gas or shrapnel,
they disappear beneath bomb-scattered rubble
they lie down and starve on stony hillsides,
being led by restful waters they slide under,
each of them another we don't have to care for

as enlivened, we stride firm sand at turn of tide,
small waves flowing to the inlet towards sundown,
from the Pacific awash benign at our right elbow;
the piled dramatic banks of cloud on the horizon
left from the set of 'Some Enchanted Evening'.

We try to conceive of our country before we came –
the inlet sandbanks crowded with pelicans, the waters
brimming with black swans and bright fish for the spearing;
cooking fires sending plumes into the soft swift dusk –
now everything left is a remnant or endangered.

Last night a large dog mauled a bird in the shallows,
perhaps a crested tern; it was distant and hard to see,
the dog plunging in foam, a white frantic wing,
a flash of red – dog's tongue or tag or bleeding wound;
the bird escaped, to struggle in the coming tide.

You know what's in my thought, the obvious thought
for one who feels more for birds than dogs – it's us.
The dog could not conceive that he did harm,
the bird was not one of him, was the merest thing,
which he savaged and cast aside without a qualm.

11. Back Home

Uluru

A caller on talkback presses – how it is wrong
to stop people climbing Uluru. When Australian men
went to fight in wars, they fought for the whole nation,
not just for the white bits, and they have a right to climb
whatever and whenever they please on Aboriginal land.
You can hear his extraordinary sense of elation,
having thought of this argument and rung to put it –
his sense of fair's fair and you've got to honour the dead,
and how the red monolith belongs to us all, and how
it is our country on which *they* make presumptuous claim.

*

Speed the day when children of Indigenous soldiers
camp on the altar steps of Christian cathedrals
or abseil the treacherous faces of the Stock Exchange
proclaiming that they fought for all Australia,
because it's theirs and they've come for a while
to enjoy the fruits of those victories (and defeats)
and a cathedral can't be sacred – it was built by men,
it is recent, untouched by the originating spirits.

Crown Land

It's not so long since the people were cajoled
for themselves and their 'Heirs and Successors'
to 'Give Grant Enfeoff and confirm unto the said
John Batman his heirs and assigns' six hundred
thousand acres of Melbourne.
                               Tomahawks
and mirrors in exchange for rivers and wide acres;
and Batman sweetened the deal with 40 blankets.

The spoilsport Governor in Sydney, intervening
on a compact freely entered by equal parties,
and there is nothing more sacred than a contract,
said the land was not the people's to trade away:
it was the Crown's and only the Crown could sell it.
Batman's swindle fell apart at the first hurdle
because a greater swindler up the line had trumped him.

I don't know what happened with the blankets.

*

Did they teach us at school that John Batman
was an unscrupulous scoundrel? No. I think
we admired his nous and shook our heads
at those who traded land for meretricious glass,
who had not looked up the law on *caveat emptor*
and had no notion of heirs and successors and assigns.
More fool them and they vanished from the story
like any other sucker or bankrupted mark.
Just so I shake my head about my great-grandfather
who fell into the Yarra and vanished from the story,
but not before he let slip what would be a fortune now –
a pasture on what became an enviable crossroad.

   And yet,
while they may justify or admire Batman's acumen,
these fellows who accuse people of swindling,
with their outrageous claims on the nation's patrimony,
and wanting to decide who enters on their property,
must somewhere, at the back of their reptilian brain,
fear that our enemy has learnt bad faith from us,
and will now pull every shameless trick and counterfeit
as revenge against us, the latest beneficiaries.

National debate

There is what they call a 'national debate' about the date
when this best little country on Earth should celebrate –

the right-thinking majority unites in decent revulsion
against the few who won't celebrate the day we took possession.

It's your style to take the piss out of us bleeding hearts
though I still don't take you for a 'like it or leave it' patriot,

but when Rosanne risks a worry about Australia Day
'they lost a war; they should get over it' you say.

Shouldn't we commemorate the day we made our peace
or like Remembrance Day when we celebrate a truce?

But no, there is no peace nor truce nor treaty, not so far;
some days it seems there never was cessation to the war.

Your words display it – there's the conquered, there's the them,
and us telling them to get used to it or we'll send the Army in.

I admit your position has its virtue; it could easily be worse –
like the claim there was no war, made by empire's apologists,

who say that only a few wrong-headed backward misfits
refused British domination and its self-evident benefits.

And seeing us as conquerors, or the heirs of conquerors, you
might allow space in the war museum for our defeated foes –

who because of their defeat have become our neighbours,
with their memories and griefs now mingled with ours.

Who gets over it, ever? Who gets over being dispossessed?
Who forgives or heals or thrives when their world is lost?

12. Great scheme

Birthday

All I knew of Syria was the persecutor Saul,
fallen in the road to Damascus when I was six,
when the Bible was felt pictures on a velvet board,
and when he got up his name was Paul.

It's your eighteenth birthday and I try to picture
a young Syrian, who opens her battered door
and steps outside, although she knows there's death
on her threshold, a good part of the time.

The best part of the time I avoid remembering
the refugees huddled on the Turkish border,
or the victims of hurricanes and mudslides,
or people on leaky boats, limping to invade us.

A great part of the time I'm carefree, like the boys
enjoying themselves in the cellars of Warsaw,
maddening their mothers by playing dive-bombers,
while in the air aboveground Stukas howled.

For a great time, I can forget the Taliban
and their devices and the soldiers we send there,
while we live safe in Melbourne and you my girl
having reached eighteen can aim for one hundred

and never to flounder as your vessel fails beneath you
or fall in the roadside and wake up a different person.

Levant

They were holiday makers, on the news, or they were idle rich,
lounging on the beachfront in civil war Beirut, and behind them
mortars explode in an apartment block and it burns, although
it is already gutted, a concrete skeleton with blank eye sockets,
and the repeated shelling seems a casual tormenting indulgence.

Their cool drinks bead the glasses in their hand, they are not
    surprised;
as if it's projected on a screen behind them, they do not flinch
    or turn;
as though they are actors who've forgotten to react
when someone else's neighbourhood is shelled to smithereens,
and ascends into their festive sky as thickening columns of smoke.

Or there is another image, from another present, from
    further north
where the two halves of Aleppo lie, one a bombed-out
    wilderness,
buildings blown to one side or another, people huddled in caverns;
and the other well-ordered, the sun radiant without filtering
    dust,
where the main grievance is the overhead boom of warplanes,
    and clatter
of choppers, on their way to blast the besieged on the other bank,
where, by day, to lead them the way, are the pillars of smoke.

Nights

It's been surprisingly easy to sleep for all the bombing
and knowing that others cannot find meals or water or doctors,
and aid agencies insist that you see those unhappy children
sleeping rough on the streets of Manila or Mogadishu.

Margaret Thatcher accused Bobby Sands of blackmail
as death closed on him, starving out of desperate conviction,
beyond helping himself, his body winding him down to extinction,
and only she could have raised him out of that appalling decline.

One Australian Prime Minister, her admirer, accused boat people
of preying upon our better nature by casting themselves on our mercy;
and another, his follower, bravely faced down the 'moral blackmail'
of the refugees we lock up and drive to suicide in the tropics,

and I confess – like every mug who elected those moral giants,
I sleep the whole night through and forget what it was I slept through.

Wine country

We were eating and drinking in the wine country this weekend,
and as I ate I calculated if it was me or themselves
they were fooling by charging so much for an unremarkable meal,
but that was not the main point, not the most difficult question.
There came a mighty wind which might have blown us off the road
on the way there or even worse on the way back, filled with costly food,
and over the ridge from our vineyard, in the next valley, a woman was killed
by a tree falling on her house and if we knew that what would we have done?
We would have finished the meal because it was pre-booked
and whether we ate it or not we would have to pick up the bill,
but we would pause and say, with a sense of good fortune,
Well did you ever! What a swell party this is!

Samaritan

He was a rhetorical figure, but the Good Samaritan plagued my mum,
as if he loomed by her wayside, putting her mercy to the test.
She would not doubt what she should do for them behind wire;
she must heed them, she could not pass by, no matter her reticence.

She, who taught me to wait my turn, who never went sneaking
after precedence, never thought of herself as important,
would not have known what to make of this dripping man
come grinning ashore from his morning swim with his minders.

He heard the cry of the desperate and turned them away,
for their own good, to prevent them drowning at sea;
and locked them up, for their own good, who had fallen
 among thieves;
but not only for them, for my good also, though I didn't ask it;

for all of us, and somehow, he squared it with the
 Parable-maker,
or not; it could be one of those evil deeds that a ruler must do,
like strangling his nephews in the tower, for the peace of the realm,
which condemns him to hell, but he must do it for the
 greater good

and the retention of power.

13. Mountain ash

Marysville

After dawn the hill frays with tatterings of clouds,
shreds drift up from the gully cut aslant
its flank. There's another hill behind, not conical,
more hunched, and forest covers both of them,
regrown the last nine years, since mountains burned.

Dead trees shimmer on the hillsides, wrecks
of burnt gums; multitudes of pallid flagstaffs
mark the contour of the crest before the fires.
Below the crest they drape the slopes with swarms
of spindly headstones, memorials of themselves.

Between me and the hills there is a stand of gums,
untouched by fire, their topsails set to catch
pale light. My watercolour pad on knee, I watch,
padded against the cold on the sodden porch –
with a paint box, a jar of water, my good brush –

I am ready to record what the mountains teach –
grey wash for clouds, diluted, serves as mist,
then I fumble for the colour of the mottled slopes,
and the overlaid effect of the stands of the dead
and botch contrasting tree tops further down.

Although it's misty every grey mast is distinct,
I scrutinise them through the brightening air.
It could be God Almighty came in majesty aflame
and burned them into signposts to the world to come,
but they turn to chaotic jumble on my page.

Erskine Falls

As we went wandering out the back of Lorne,
blurred by fog and the uproar of the falls,
the cliff-top trees were misted spectres,
gesturing through drifts of filmy light,
and in that blue bushwalker's raincoat
you flickered eerie on my edge of sight.

It was the raincoat of my wife before you,
who wore it on a forest track past Lorne –
slender woman, ballooning from her treatment.
I fear she refrained from telling me her fear
for dread that mine would torrent into hers
and flood her desperate calm. Unlike the ash,
whose quiet descended to her from the crests,
I was a cracked bell jangling with distress.

There's one last favour that I'll ask of you –
pull on that blue raincoat, drive me there
to Turton's Track, let me breathe the ancient air,
and back to Erskine Falls, if my legs don't fail.

I will stand silent, thrown over by the rush
of wind gusts in the stands of mountain ash,
and try to freeze the cascade in its drop
by following one bead of spray from top
to bottom of the falls, trick time to stop.

Your hair's bejewelled with droplets of the Falls;
through the ragged tops the high mist swirls.

Dropping the wires

In the vineyard John and I are dropping wires – unclip them,
then clip them lower on the post, then check the nails in clips,
then check the staple holding the cordon, where there twist
the outspread arms and elbows of the vine; then to the next post.

Donald Trump is getting close to Hilary Clinton (in the polls)
and I foresee a world with him in charge; it will be wild,
like pulling the carpet from beneath the Western World,
I guess, stumbling over ripped soil between the rows.

The wind is rising in the vines; the spring surge just come on them,
their young leaves still bright, they send out tendrils with vegetal cunning;
it's a crime against nature to break a shoot as you snap wires in place,
although you calculate – with that many shoots will one less hurt? –

But each gentle winding strand is beauteous in the eye of heaven,
and as for the tender inflorescences, from which the grapes will grow,
their close-bunched green buds touched with a dust of vermilion,
each of them is too precious to damage with a brush of glove.

The vine rows trace the hillside's curve and at the bottom of each row
you look along the line at an eternity of endless posts.
This is what salvation must be like, after a while, you suppose.
Bob Dylan has announced that he'll accept the Nobel Prize.

When the wind gusts, it whistles lightly in the vines; the
    wires ping
with a metallic zing, like a quick-bent saw blade as you let the
    tension go;
John's hammer-blows in the next row spread across an
    expanse of air,
it sounds like he is working on a slope far across the shallow valley.

For hours on end we don't talk, just wind rushing around my ears
and crows considering loudly which of my bones they will
    pick first;
but the loudest sound is the malevolent chatter of the cockatoos,
set to come marauding sometime soon on the sweet new shoots.

There's a wide sky stacked above us high with silent cloud;
beyond Glenrowan Gap the sky flares like imminent Ascension;
vine leaves whisper with the first drops of rain, and there's
a faint drumming as the shower sweeps over broken soil.

Below, beyond, our human wavelength, the great earth sighs.

14. Broken Head

The tree is not there

This soon after the event, they're making a movie of the murder.
They tell me I'm required to act my own part from that night.
I once played a hooded priest at a hanging and I haven't asked
but I hope the pay is good, especially with that prior experience.

The tram trip to the scene goes well, though we don't start from the right stop,
and the stop we start from seems classier, better lit, than the right one,
and the advertising posters seem directed to a better class of patron.
I make no comment; they're filmmakers and it could be product placement.

When we get there, it seems darker and more sinister than the first time.
It was a huge open shed with trams and buses under orange floodlights,
now it's ramshackle and grainy, the floodlights changed for feeble bulbs.
A scriptwriter has heightened things; as if it wasn't alarming the first time.

Nothing is the same as it was, but everything trundles along until the crew
takes me to the front of the prime mover and the tree is not there.
It had been dragged for miles and was a dead giveaway on the night,
shedding a sharp light on the identity of either the driver or the killer.

I keep a straight face. I won't mention the critical missing
 eucalypt;
they may have left out the tree on purpose to see how I deal
 with it –
the mountain ash with mud and the scraps of cloth caught in
 its leaves,
with the telltale white powdered surface of juvenile foliage.

If they know the tree was there and I don't react they'll suppose
I have something to hide and come down on me like a tonne
 of bricks,
because I'm sure the cops are watching a live-feed, and this is
 a set-up
to prove I was guilty or to prove I wasn't there, which I was as
 far as I recall.

Broken Head

Gannets have gone berserk for feeding –
dive wildly, steadying wings half-spread
until the instant they slice surface.

It is aerial mayhem, free-for-all,
each makes hay while its sun shines,
combined they pin the shoal against the bluff.

Off the long beach south of Byron,
wet-suited surfers speckled near the point,
scores of sea birds plunder teeming bait.

First the terns, small-bodied, dark-faced,
their wingtips on the downstroke almost
touching in swift unstudied elegance,

and when we walk back an hour later,
the gannets, bigger, have ejected them;
more daredevil even than the terns.

Three plummet from the whirling,
breakneck through the wave-face,
three pagan godlings on the pillage

who maraud without forethought,
murder without malice,
and die leaving nothing undone.

Nothing but eternal peace

Behind my back the stealthy dawn turns day to light.
The world outside can wait; I face the dark and write.

Bad sky at night

A threat of storm rages ragged from the south
into clear sky, shining dead ahead, above the trees;
while nearer, pale skeins catch the light, sail on,
as though no stark catastrophe is near at hand.

Anti-aircraft pom-poms are fading to the right: like
a lone plane broke away for the last patch of sky,
its flimsy wingtips waggling semaphore as it ran,
silhouetted, through the gauntlet to receding light.

The vanishing tint of gold, or maybe apricot, has leached
from the radiance; all that's left is a pewter undertone
and streaks, like you've dragged a brush of bluish grey
dry across wet silver-white, or the other way around.

It's the sort of scene they print on science fiction,
evoking perilous lands, a long way from our star –
shipwrecked on a planet, where black rollers break forlorn
and I stand one out like a violin against the crash of brass.

Saint-Exupéry flew reconnaissance just above the reach
of German guns, above Arras, dreamy for lack of oxygen,
half in love with the shells that bloomed about his plane,
and lived, to fly across to near Marseille, and disappear.

Who makes this stuff up?

I dreamed I turned one hundred. Part of me wanted that:
the obscure ill-wisher who jeers at my dishevelled continuance,
at the drive built in my sinews to shuffle on, regardless;
treacherous, upending me naked before enemies and friends,
satirical about my vainest small ambition, like the failed wish
to do one completed stylish thing, the once, with no doubt
about the moral worth or weight of the attempt for beauty.

I had turned one hundred but dragged myself to work –
no one took much notice of my birthday at the office,
me being known to few, shabby and unremarkable,
the inoffensive sucker they wheel in because someone
dispensable is required to obsess over old disasters.

One hundred is a barren, cursed place – it is too late
to be promising, no greatness lies ahead, the past is done –
too late to be fancy or meticulous, to learn new chords,
or return to works you left for when you could perfect them –
the sketches of Lake Gard, puzzled versions of French poets.

Nothing but eternal peace

The Sorgue flows a long time lightless underground,
emerges in a rush above Fontaine-de-Vaucluse,
glistens past the Musée de la Résistance in a mill.
The wheel no longer turns but deep inside you walk
in the subdued light of faintest memory and lost causes.

We went there once, it came instantly to mind,
when Sebald's Austerlitz tells how his Marie recalled
a mill and waters of a deep, unnatural green,
where the ripple of moving water soothes, and wood
creaks as sluicing waters in the race revolve the wheel,
where the mote-filled air is stripped with beams of light
crept through wooden slats into the muffled gloom,
and where she wished for 'nothing more but eternal peace'.

Soon though, I know, I would begin to starve for love,
or for a lake with pale cliffs facing from the other shore.

Pale cliffs

Night is pulling out; it draws westward over mountains;
faint dawn can't disperse the dark still on the lake
streaked with shaken glimmers of the streetlights of Salò.

The high cliffs opposite are pallid shadows but the peaks
behind them catch an early flare of sun and incandesce;
nearer, half-formed ridges struggle vaguely toward being.

On the balcony, chilled, peering through sleeplessness,
sketchpad on the table and a pencil in my hand, I should
forget myself and let the pencil take itself about the page.

It would be great just once to find a drawing flows,
not this trail left in the gloom by a semi-conscious hand,
on a subject too grand for my talent to command.

A sob disorders me, it is threatening my line – a gulp
ascending from my glacier-carved depths, to shake me
with regret or thankfulness – to have made it here, so late.

You move behind me in the unlit house, speak soft;
stealthily I swipe the corner of my eye. You brought me
to this dawn, secretly lightening the pale rock with rose.

To RC framed in a prospect of vines

In these fields of vines and wires I've knocked myself out –
hefting the water drill, boring planting holes, wrestling
it into gravel resistant; and then the only morning
I spent picking was hell, was like to make an end of me.

Mostly I stand witless while others shout commands
around the sheds. I must exercise a special vigilance
to ensure that I don't do anything that a child,
even, would blush at, and I hope that like the dogs
I get out of the way of grown-ups when it counts.
But there was that time you came here with me,
when I stumbled through rough grass to try one grape
from the lustrous clusters on the vines and the boss
says to you 'he looks at home'; which was, strangely, right.

Anyone who stands beside the mass of vines in summer,
as they transubstantiate in silence, sway in solar wind,
will gain another lovely green dimension: as you did.
I looked at you there and saw the straight-limbed woman
who walked before me through the malbec vineyards
on open slopes, where pilgrim pathways straggle
through landscape left over from the Hundred Years War,
where we stopped to test a tart grape.

                                        You are home,
a gentlewoman still abed this Sunday morning, and I doubt
you'll count it a misfortune not to be with me, up early
on the vine-clad slopes of Everton, where I await my battle
with press, pumps and hoses, must and juice and pressings
and the plastic shovel come adrift from its broken handle,
but I count it my bad luck not to be with you, wherever,
in any Sunday bed you choose, to do as you command.

Limone

The road to Limone forks hard left, but we drove on
not knowing Lawrence lived there, many weeks,
writing his contorted theories into travelogue.

One morning he watched a winter sunrise on Lake Gard –
looking eastwards, whilst I looked to the west in spring,
him warm abed and me up chilly at an earlier hour.

He saw the sun fire up a strip of light along the ridge
and finally arise above an indigo peak, snow-capped,
blazing a trail across the milky lightening waters.

That would be Monte Baldi where we sped above
the swaying woods and clearings in a fraught gondola
to the alpine crest, which had borne Laurentian snow.

We looked southward down the lake at misting time –
golden afternoon up here while across the distant lake
a vaporous haze of light dropped from the milky blue.

The stirring progress of the far-flung lake's attendant
peaks and sudden cliffs, vanished in a blitz of dazzlement;
we stood against the gusts as on the edge of flight.

The trails above Castelletto

Mild airs at lakeside in the dusk and cool
when I wake by still water before dawn;

we labour up stone alleys through the shade,
break free onto the brilliant hillside high
above our lakeside town

                            – tawdry, touristed,
beset, by the short-tempered snarl of holiday cars,
it looks a peaceful village seen from here
above Castelletto at the end of spring:

faded sunlight flickers through unkempt olive trees,
shrines to the Virgin fade by rocky paths along the hills,
the bright lake glitters from down the dappled breakneck slopes;

beyond the great cliffs opposite, arise
the godly hulks of shrouded mountains.

Sweet and low, secret breezes satin on my skin;
I am basin-brimming with trickled gladness,
then gladness overspills to thankfulness, and then
being thankful flows to wondering who or what
to thank for being glad, as if belief is built in me,
as if the physical world lives and for some purpose,
on the trails above Castelletto, close to summer.

Mausoleum

The Good Shepherd tends His sheep as radiant as though
they were uplifted, peaceful, to their lunette yesterday;
two stags have caught their antlers in elaborate shrubs:
wandered in, they find they must remain and pray;

an endless ribbon winds on arches holding up the sky;
the sprawling universe of scattered stars comes down
and prints a patterned swirl of constellations on the dome;
flowers like snowflakes burst on fields of lapis lazuli.

Dante Square

Dante has taken refuge in Verona; gloom on a pedestal.
Italy's united, kind of; we all speak Tuscan, sort of;
and he soared to the Empyrean and lived to tell the tale
to the prince whose palace blazes here with electric lamps.
There is no cause for gloom, but he hunches in his cloak
as glamorous women saunter in the palace colonnades.

A girl teaches her younger sister ballet at Dante's plinth;
they stumble, rearrange their limbs, and try again.
There's a busker with an accordion and an amp on wheels
who plays tunes from the movies with a rough panache;
an attractive woman sweet-talks for a ringside seat,
and fondly children, dogs and friends greet friends.

With a sling a pedlar shoots a glowing arrow in the sky
which whirls, slantwise, back into his outstretched hand.
The flying arrow makes itself a centre of the dusk;
as silent and portentous as a solitary flare which drifts
above the Harbour before the New Year's fireworks start,
as if a mosaic flame took flight across a lapis lazuli field.

Day draws beyond the pediments, retreats into the upper air –
it is not that darkness falls, it is that we lose the light.

In the springtime

All the afternoon, which was a turmoil of crowdedness,
you would disappear with him and return with another tale
of someone being boorish or abominable to each of you
and I would ask for details earnestly, as if I believed it all.

You went off on some errand and left me to speak with him.
I had to seem oblivious or far above your mean intrigue
but you returned and smiled and said 'Two likely lads'
and it was hard to retain my semblance of self-control.

That's when I saw you lead your friend up a grassy bank
your arm outstretched to take him by the hand; you glanced
back at him with a frank affection which I know full well
having been sometime the focus of that lovely beam myself.

'That's that,' I moaned, soon desolation would crash down,
I would be wretchedly adrift and hollow as a flotsam cask;
but in this moment, I suffered a kind of rejoicing, you were
the life in me, I knew your love; always it was going to end.

Dream of defeat #23

A dolphin drifting languorous to the air
for a toke of consciousness before
sinking again into the sleeping depths,
is as awake as I was, when you spoke.

I am Nebuchadnezzar, groaning in an opera
bellowing how my mud-brick cities crumble;
spare me your lamentation, pity earth,
for with my fall the firmament is wracked.

You prophets sifting the fire-cracked bones
of beasts you murder on your altar stones,
who divined that I must end calamitous,
your temple columns start to tremble.

Cast out by my subjects, a ruined tramp,
I shambled spindle-shins towards
a rundown house, geraniums in pots,
which might give refuge to a toppled king.

So yes, my wakeful love, I am awake.

A source

By a former paper mill in the Vaucluse, the Sorgue,
new-freed, runs fast and clear but unnatural green,
from the water weed, unripe lemon, shining through;
channels within the rock drag snowmelt from Ventoux
to where it gushes from the limestone in full spate.
We walked to the source, then back for lunch, by green.

It was true then – the underground river below the mansion
of Bruce Wayne, which seemed too marvellous to believe,
spilling dim through caverns measureless to man.

Batman does not have the same pull in your life.
You're of an age to have seen the TV shows and films
but not the real, the glorious, gravely printed myths
where I turned for learning on the law and crime and how
each meek man worth his salt has a double he keeps hid,
who should spring out when the chips are going down.

I saw the TV show, its tongue in cheek, its BIFFs and POWs,
its plots facetiously incredible and my thought was like
my father exclaiming to my mother when he first heard
the Flamingos sing *I only have eyes for you* –
      Sh'bup, sh'bup
bouncing to eternity like a moth between two mirrors –
'Would you believe what they've done to this one, Jo?'

I knew no other version of the song, and this one, sung
in a dripping cavern way under Gotham City,
with a studio hand gone mad with the reverb machine,
dragged me deep with the singer made blind by love.

Faintest memory and lost causes

May 2019

Below the ruined fort and its tower on the rocky ridge,
deep in the flood-cut gorge, by the paper mill on the Sorgue,
the proprietor's son, Jean Garcin, was recruited to resist
and began selecting comrades from about, who became
assassins and saboteurs, bombers and armed guards
for the meetings and the high officials of the Résistance.

Absurdly, a sedentary gradualist, I feel that I am with them,
not as brave and not at all at risk, and not hard-pressed –
bound to their country but hating what it had become,
they lived a hope of liberation which made them outcast,
caught in a state which rejected them and hunted them
with a deadly scorn, as enemies of good order, and the good.

They didn't get their France, the one they fought for.
The war was won, and the filthy flood of normality rolled back.
The high ideals, how it would not be business as corruptly usual,
how we would deal with each other squarely, respecting
mutual need, common sacrifice, the sharing of fears and hopes,
all swept away; the manoeuvrers won again. Like here, now.

We owe him everything

At a gallery on the quai d'Orfèvres, near Notre Dame,
a few steps from the astonishing Sainte-Chapelle,
Daniel[4] was sent off to view Kandinsky's recent works,
which he found childlike but also disconcerting,
while the boss talked art or resistance with the owner.

He does not write of St Louis' entrancing church;
perhaps art for him in wartime was a trivial distraction,
but also, Sainte-Chapelle had lost its brilliant glory –
the stained glass taken down in case of air raids or defeat,
to prevent the loss of those fragments of blue heaven.

That was three weeks before the boss was betrayed
and captured, in a suburban doctor's house near Lyon,
and weeks later he would die on the Berlin train,
despatched by Klaus Barbie, as a trophy, comatose;
but he spent that night in Paris talking modern art.

With their gallery business done they walked along the *quai*
and then across Pont Neuf towards the Métro, Saint-Michel,
where we first emerged in Paris, blinking into daylight
by the morning Seine, trundling cantankerous luggage
across cobbles away towards the top of Rue Mazarine,

the art stalls on the embankment unfurling their canvases
and the shutters on the cafés coming down or rolling up,
with the homeless stiffly moving out of cluttered doorways,
gipsy tricksters sauntering to their pitch, and across the Seine
the buildings on the quai d'Orfèvres, not that we knew that.

Somewhere here they dined, and Moulin gave him a book
with De Chirico and Cézanne in black and white;
then Jean Moulin turned again to talking of Cézanne,
'he gave us modern art', he said, knowing Daniel's aversions,
but giving the kid a chance – 'we owe him everything'.

As if art, or modern art, or Cézanne, was all their cause,
as if what they fought for, Daniel and he, was Cézanne,
a morose southerner who would never paint straight,
and fled south to dodge conscription in the Prussian war,
where, fleeing duty, he was seized by passion for his work.

*

I seek out Cézanne's watercolour studies of Provence –
this one of *Trees by Water*, on a winter morning,
the soft vacancies of mists and pale reflections failing
to ripple the chill surface, rendered with adept love;
or these trees *In the Woods* with the colour brushed

in translucent swatches through the sketched-in trees –
warm yellow highlights, violet for the depths of shade,
at the overlaps the colours blend their luminosities,
as if the woods dissolved into a play of summer light,
or the holy glaziers of Sainte-Chappelle returned.

Painting white

All week I've painted white, coat after coat of it,
after sanding at a sprawl of ham-fisted marks –
repriming canvases to revive them from marred starts.

I work towards the utmost seductive blankness,
these surfaces will brim with wonders that might be –
they will shine at me with unblemished promises.

Though I make each blank, each one contains its past,
I know what lies beneath. The larger canvas
started as a stand of eucalypts past Healesville;

that day was immense, great gusts of wind made sure
you knew your place and that your place was minuscule,
a tree would fall and drop you dead at any moment;

the other was from an old friend's photo of the Edwards –
a woolshed doorway frames a view of bush and water,
pretty as a Heysen picture until I got to work on it.

All the while, over days, I fantasise the next step,
like a football commentary in my head, what I will do,
the bumbler somehow flukes a miraculous mark;

for now, my aim is two Platonic quadrilaterals,
to be the Forms of every other untouched shape,
as perfect as the circle Giotto drew for Cimabue.

Ruination

They suggest the fires are like Egypt's seven plagues, sent
to teach us we're the best little country on Earth,
because we pull together in a crisis, help each other out,
as though self-congratulation is worth a score of lives.

It gets inside me; it fills me full of woe, this chemical-thick
murk above the Harbour, dense so you can't see hills,
or treetops, or the wake of ferries as they vanish,
bearing the best little people to the invisible North Shore.

The same blokes keep telling me that ours is a hard land
where disasters are always happening, and we will cope –
as though bushfires were volcanos, nothing can be done,
but they would say that, to excuse deliberate neglect.

I can't shake this sense that we brought this on ourselves,
but I never voted for this vacant scoundrel who believes
he can wait it out – that we'll forget that he soothed and lied
and pulled accounting tricks proving nothing need be done.

I repent every lung of CO_2 I've launched into the air,
and I hope my little sister who deserves to be kept safe,
will not be burned out. She didn't vote for him either
but apart from that, what harm has she ever done?

Here's a misery of smoke sent in by ruined country;
soon we'll breath red dust lifted from denuded farms.
It gets inside me, woefully; although it's only atmosphere
it feels like something worse, a fundamental worsening.

We cannot say what it was

The row of empties grows upon the packing cartons
brought from the Rhone and Sicily and Piedmont
and from Yarra valley, which tonight will fall to freezing

while Jim tells his tales from Papua, on the Kokoda track,
pressed beyond his bodily limits, plumbing agonies of exhilaration;
swept up by singers who learned harmony in church,

then ripped from it to wander among us lost and mourning,
and although the rest of us have not endured a test as
    punishing as his
we all have scaled a pinnacle and been required to redescend

to this sad world beneath the pragmatic sun, and when we
    attempt to transport
words from the other world, as in Canada they carry their
    canoes from lake to lake,
even as we utter them, they slip from our grasp; not even the
    word for loss will float.

Flags

In memory of Terry Monagle

The first monk said, 'The flag is moving.'
The second said, 'It is the wind that moves.'
The master, who was passing, said,
Not the wind, not the flag, the mind is moving.

Zen monks are only fall-guys for the master,
but the first monk's self-propelling flag provokes,
more puzzling than a flag moved by the mind:
Not the wind, not the mind, the flag is moving.

You feared that without faith the world lacks depth,
although your way of putting it implies
that it's you who fuses faith into your world –
withdraw your breath of faith, the flag falls slack.

Once you felt that tearing off your shirt
would be enough to let transcendence in,
but wherever glory ends, it starts from you.
Air touches skin and radiance ensues.

Meek man, no double

Thursday night, outside Trades Hall,
two, drunk, kicking, on the ground,
slumped at our white-collar feet,
one lost soul, who screams –
no other word will do.

About to go our own three ways
we found him fallen at our toes,
nearly tripped, then stepped over,
which left us facing two drunk men
who hadn't had their fill of kicking,
rage burned like a brazier before them.

They stare, they move to pass around us –
'Come on, mate, you've kicked him enough,'
I say, and shift from foot to shaking foot,
trying to hold his weaving eye, and hope
that does not become a provocation.

I'm tall, he doesn't like the look of that,
the booze has stuffed his frontal lobe,
he sways like an automaton whose
balancing flywheel has run amok.
My height might save me one more time.

Religion and the second bass

Never want to be a tenor, apple of too many eyes,
the strained plaintive, the quavering whinge,
the certainty that what they're feeling must be prized.
I would do 'Go Down Moses' in the shower and plunge
for the lowest note, on 'Pharaoh', and after nights
of smoking I could growl it with a roughened edge.

But my certainty, my moment of conversion, came
when I heard a bass sing the Gospel in a Russian church.
I do not know which passage from which Evangelist
but roaming Galilee had put hairs upon his chest:
that was the real sublime, forget your angelic choirs;
battering, urgent, a voice from utterly below, mounts
to another overpowering bass note with each phrase:

it's a long tsunami driven by an earthquake from Peru,
it's the rumble of mountains rising from the clash of plates,
the catastrophic roar of stars foundering in black holes,
this is the intolerable booming of brass-throated God.

Night, Córdoba

A royal water garden, jets and pools,
glitters unseen to our left, below
the ridge that lifts us into midnight,
born upon mild airs among dim stars.

The singer slouches forward in his chair
not seeing us, but with his inward eye
stares upon long-nurtured slights.
At verse-end he gives one derisive clap

and negligently lets the two guitarists loose
to blaze into the dark, while he re-stokes
his scorn; they're good, they're way too good;
I ache with envying these blessed youths.

Some songs seize him with a furious dejection:
I cannot guess what outrage makes him turn
his back on us, to shrug and walk offstage;
but clearly, he's a noble, mistreated man.

You sleep on my shoulder, fountains splash;
wild horses trample in my docile breast:
If those were my fingers on the strings!
And those my songs – proud, unreconciled.

Il penseroso III

Hooligan storm jumps me in the dark,
thunder rumbling down the aerial rails,
heading for the tinpot local hills;
squalls uproot the nearest avenues,
rip off rooves and frisbee trampolines.

My daughter studies late tonight.
I think of Yeats who thought of Milton
at work in his tower by candlelight,
one small inconstant point of flame
feeble against the hurling dark.

On a night maybe worse than this
he prayed his daughter may be spared
from the blustering Atlantic blast;
but a whirlwind splintered through
my daughter's life when she was two.

I am not yet fool or cowed enough
to seek mercy from the merciless
for me, but for my child? I beg
that at last she'll sleep this night,
hold fast against the buffeting.

Yeats wished for his child a life
of custom and of ceremony, but I lack
the innocence to ask for that for mine;
we're tossed, we fight to stay upright,
we stagger in the street of gales.

Bad night at Blois

Last night was bad in that coffin room in Paris,
with the lass next door coming through the wall.
What French cunning contrived her moaning bliss?
And what will I do if you demand the same?
Blois, I bet, boasts no such cruel hotel, but

no Blois doctor will attend me, our host regrets,
me not being French, which leaves me bereft,
akin to Dante, fevered by Venetian marsh,
and all distempered poets, laid low and sweating,
in pilgrim cell or tapestry-smothered hall.

The lady they pursued and tuned high love for,
they can't recall the sacred name they gave her,
nor the glisten of her flesh beneath their fingers,
nor conjure the emptiest gesture of desire;
coughing filthily on some straw-strewn floor.

Our gizzards of a room in Blois contracts,
and I smother every whimper of a cough,
certain something great depends on that –
our marriage, sure, imperilled by your rage
against my racking, sleep-despatching hack:

but something more – this cough which jars
my brain, which talons at my flooded lungs,
could jag the netted fabric of space/time,
undo its whole fine-woven filament,
and I'd be left staring wildly at the dark.

No dead soul, not even Saints, will gaze
upon God's face before the Judgement Day,
according to Pope John, who Dante reviles,
not naming names for once, for other crimes,
but there'll be no *Paradiso* if John's right.

This Pope barges upstream on the Rhone,
falls deathly sick at a town called Valréas,
is cured by their wine and buys the town
so he will never be without – he's in no rush
to prove when he'll view God face to face.

Dad, you've come! Not even the grave
makes you more pallid than when last we met
when you paused long between each jagged breath
and I felt I attended on an ancient king
who must do the weightiest deed he'd ever do.

And mum, doing what a child fears most:
you turn away, absorbed by your great task,
your fingers telling rosary, your breath hoarse,
doing alone what you alone can do,
although, faithless, I pray Hail Marys for you.

Both gone before; may I make as brave a fist;
but here in Blois, with a long bike ride ahead
and my head aflame with this deathly grippe,
I shake with a melodramatic dread,
and like Pope John I'm not eager for the test.

Notes

1. George Orwell, 'Looking back at the Spanish War', 1943, reprinted with *Homage to Catalonia*, Penguin, 1966.

   The pious ones, from the Pope to the yogis of California, are great on the 'change of heart', much more reassuring from their point of view than a change in the economic system. Petain attributes the fall of France to the common people's 'love of pleasure'. One sees this in its right perspective if one stops to wonder how much pleasure the ordinary French peasant's or working-man's life would contain compared with Petain's own. The damned impertinence of these politicians, priests, literary men, and what-not who lecture the working-class socialist for his 'materialism'! All that the working man demands is what these others would consider the indispensable minimum without which human life cannot be lived at all. Enough to eat, freedom from the haunting terror of unemployment, the knowledge that your children will get a fair chance, a bath once a day, clean linen reasonably often, a roof that doesn't leak, and short enough working hours to leave you with a little energy when the day is done. Not one of those who preach against 'materialism' would consider life liveable without these things.

2. René Char, *Feuillets d'Hypnos*, from Fragment 138 (my translation and line breaks). This event took place at Céreste, about thirty kilometres from Saint-Saturnin-lès-Apt on 22 June 1944, ten days before the killings at Saint-Saturnin-lès-Apt.

3. The fourteen dead at Saint-Saturnin-lès-Apt, Vaucluse, 1 July 1944 were as follows.

- Brought by a party of SS and collaborationist militia from Cavaillon and shot before dawn on the rocks at Romanet: Isaac Malho, 31, born in Athens; Albert Rouzeau, 21, from Hérault; Maurice Barthou, 26, resident of Cavaillon; two unknown men.
- Killed in the dawn attack on the ruined farm at Gayéoux further on from Romanet and before Berre: Lucien Moulinas, 21, from Orgon, a town further south; Guy Planchenault, a sous-lieutenant, 20, from Saint Jean de Luz in the German 'forbidden zone' on the Atlantic coast close to the Spanish border; Lucien Crespo, 17, from Robion near Cavaillon; Roger Moureau, nearly 20, from Malakoff a locality of Paris south of Montparnasse.
- Blanche Gaillard was shot at her farm at Berre in the early morning.
- Executed in the square at Saint-Saturnin-lès-Apt at about 1 p.m.: Paulette Nouveau, 31, of Gordes (captured at Berre); and three men who surrendered at Gayéoux – Armel Collet, 19, from Lagnes a few kilometres north of Robion; Jean Fossier, 18, from Robion; Robert le Belge.

4. Daniel Cordier, *Alias Caracalla*, p. 846. On 27 May 1943, three weeks before the Germans captured him, Jean Moulin, who was de Gaulle's personal representative to the Résistance, looked through a book of black and white reproductions with Daniel Cordier, who was his young personal assistant.

> He looked for reproductions of De Chirico and then returned to the first pages: 'This is Cezanne, who I've often spoken about to you. Examine his works carefully. He is the most important, even if one loves the other Impressionists. He founded modern art. We owe him everything.'

About the Author

David Bunn grew up on the Mornington Peninsula in Victoria. He was schooled there and then studied at the University of Melbourne.

He worked in Australian white-collar trade unions for forty years, in Sydney and Melbourne.

He has had poetry published in anthologies associated with the Montreal International Poetry Prize (2011 and 2015); in *Long Glances*, the anthology associated with the 2013 Jean Cecily Drake-Brockman Poetry Prize; and in the *Australian Poetry Anthology* (2015 and 2020). He was joint winner of the Gwen Harwood prize in 2012 and that poem appeared in *Island*. *The Great Scheme* is the first book of his verse to be published.

He now lives in Melbourne.

www.ingramcontent.com/pod-product-compliance
Lightning Source LLC
Chambersburg PA
CBHW070931080526